Tell me . .

. . . about the
Lord Jesus Christ

2

Tell me ...
... about the
Lord Jesus Christ

DEREK PRIME

KINGSWAY PUBLICATIONS
EASTBOURNE

This series based on 'Tell me the answer'
books which were first published in 1965.
This new series © Derek Prime 1975

Reprinted 1979

ISBN 0 85476 234 5

Illustrations and cover design
by Elsie Sands

Printed in Great Britain for
KINGSWAY PUBLICATIONS LTD.,
Lottbridge Drove, Eastbourne, E. Sussex BN23 6NT
by Fletcher & Son Ltd, Norwich

I

Robert comes to stay

Very early on Sunday morning the telephone rang. Stephen and Joanna Price heard their father go downstairs to answer it. They guessed by the way that he was talking that there was bad news.

"Yes," they heard him say, "we shall be glad to have Robert stay here. Why don't you let him come today, after the morning service? Then you can leave for Scotland early on Monday ... Yes, that will be fine."

Stephen and Joanna were not sure who their father was speaking to. They knew only one Robert, and he was the four-year-old son of friends at their church. As their father came up the stairs, they couldn't contain their curiosity.

"Daddy, we heard you talking about Robert. Was it Robert Fyson?"

"Yes," answered Mr. Price. "Mr. and Mrs. Fyson have just had some bad news. Mr. Fyson's elderly mother died suddenly during the night up in Scotland. Mr. Fyson feels that he and Mrs. Fyson must go up as soon as possible to help his father do all the things that need to be done. Mr. Fyson was wondering whether Robert could stay with us for a few days—it might be as long as a week. Of course, I said yes. So Robert's coming after morning service. I hope he won't be too homesick."

"We'll do our best to help him not to be," promised Joanna. "It'll be fun having someone younger to play with. He can play with our toys when we're at school, can't he, Steve?"

"Yes," nodded Stephen, "as long as he's careful. Hey, it's Harvest Thanksgiving at church today. I'm looking forward to it."

"I'd forgotten that for a moment," Mr. Price said. "Have you got your things ready to put on the Sunday School's tables?"

"Mine are all packed in a little basket the greengrocer gave me, Dad," explained Joanna. "Steve's taking tinned stuff, so his is in a carrier bag."

*   *   *

They could tell it was harvest as soon as they went through the church doors.

"What a lovely smell!" exclaimed Joanna.

"Doesn't it look fabulous?" added Stephen.

There were flowers and vegetables, fruit and tins of all sorts of things. It looked as if several greengrocers and grocers had brought everything in their shops into the church!

"Look at that loaf in the middle, Steve. Isn't it huge?"

"And all those spuds! Wow, Jo, I've never seen so many!"

Mr. and Mrs. Fyson and Robert came and sat next to the Prices; together they nearly filled the whole row. The children enjoyed singing the harvest hymns, especially 'We plough the fields and scatter the good seed on the land', which was their favourite. Robert couldn't read yet, but he knew the chorus, 'All good gifts around us', and he joined in very loudly when the time came to sing it.

* * *

Robert didn't seem unhappy about leaving his parents. He liked being with Stephen and Joanna, because they played with him and read him stories.

After tea, Mrs. Price approached the difficult subject of bedtime. "I think, Robert, you must go up to bed at six o'clock, because your mummy said that was your usual time."

"Will the twins go then, too?" Robert asked, a hint of tears coming to his eyes.

"Well, no. They'll go a little later because they're older."

"I don't want to go to bed on my own," complained Robert; the tears were very near now.

"I'll tell you what," said Joanna. "Mummy will read you a Bible story before you go to bed, and Steve and I will come up with you and listen to it as well. How's that?"

Robert nodded his head, a little mournfully.

"Get undressed first, then, Robert, and as soon as you're in your pyjamas and washed, we'll have the story in your bedroom."

The story Robert chose was the feeding of the five thousand with the little boy's lunch of loaves and fishes. When Mrs. Price had finished reading it, she exclaimed, "That was a good story to choose, Robert, on Harvest Sunday! Making the loaves and fishes go such a long way was what we call a miracle. But it was easy for the Lord Jesus because He is God, and He made everything."

"Yes, Mummy," added Joanna. "In Sunday School this morning we were told the Lord Jesus made all the harvest gifts we could see in church—even the metal for the tins for the baked beans!"

"Did Jesus really make everything?" asked Robert.

"Yes, everything. All the wonderful gifts we see at harvest were made by the Lord Jesus Christ." She remembered Robert's singing in the morning service. "Let's sing 'All good gifts', shall we?"

A big smile appeared on Robert's face as they sang together

'All good gifts around us
Are sent from heaven above;
Then thank the Lord, O thank the Lord,
For all His love.'

"I like singing," Robert said. "Can we sing something else?"

"Yes, of course, in a minute."

Robert kicked his feet against the bed. "What did Jesus look like?"

"I don't really know," answered Mrs. Price.

"I do," said Robert knowingly. "I've seen a picture of Him at Sunday School."

"That's only imagined, silly," interrupted Stephen.

"No, he isn't silly, Steve," Mrs. Price corrected. "Robert's right. Many artists have drawn pictures of Jesus and you can see them in story books. But you must remember that the artists are only guessing what Jesus looks like. They might be right or they might not."

"I'm sure He looks very kind," said Joanna. "The sort of person I like to have as a friend."

"I'm sure you're right, Jo," agreed her mother. "The Bible doesn't give us a photograph of Jesus. But it does something much better—it tells us the kind of person Jesus is. It tells us that Jesus is perfect, loving and kind—the best friend a boy or girl can have. Who's your best friend at school, Steve?"

Stephen didn't have to think very long before he replied, "Chris Green."

"Why is he your best friend?"

Stephen thought for a moment. "Well, he shares things; he never lets you down or tells tales about you; and he likes doing the same things I do."

"Then he isn't your best friend because of what he looks like?" enquired his mother.

"Of course not!" exclaimed Stephen. "That doesn't matter."

"Then you can see why the Bible doesn't tell us what the Lord Jesus looks like," continued Mrs. Price, "but why it tells us instead the kind of person Jesus is. He's the best person who has ever lived on this earth. He was always kind, and never let anyone down. And He died to save His friends."

"We shall see Jesus one day though, won't we, Mum? The Bible says so, when He comes again."

"Yes, Jo," agreed her mother. "That will be a wonderful day."

They were interrupted by a loud yawn; Mrs.

Price realised that Robert could hardly keep his eyes open.

"Into bed, sleepy head!"

When Robert had finally been bundled into bed, Stephen and Joanna noticed he was looking miserable again, and guessed he was missing his own home and his parents. Mrs. Price helped Robert to say his prayers, and they asked the Lord Jesus to keep Robert safe until morning and to bless his father and mother.

Mrs. Price was just about to switch off the light when Robert asked, "If you close the curtains, Jesus can't see me, can He?"

She smiled. "Yes, He can, Robert. Jesus is God, and He sees and knows everything. Nothing happens anywhere without His knowing all about it. So He is always able to keep us safe. He sees me, and He sees Stephen and Joanna, and He sees your Mummy and Daddy too. And He watches over us all. He never wants us to be lonely; He always stays with us."

"Even when we've been naughty and disobedient," added Joanna.

"Well, Jo, the Lord Jesus doesn't leave us, but we don't please Him when we sin. If we're truly sorry, He'll forgive us, and help us to do better. Jesus is the best friend you can have. He will hear even when you whisper to Him."

"I know a chorus about that," Robert remembered.

"So do we," Stephen and Joanna chimed in together.

"All right," suggested Mrs. Price, "let's sing it together before we say 'Good night'."

> 'School days, play days, sad days, gay days;
> Sunshine or wet days; whate'er you get days;
> "Never alone", my Saviour is near;
> Even a whisper He will hear.'

"Good night, Robert. I'll buy you a Bible colouring book tomorrow morning. Then you can colour it while the twins are at school, and we'll talk about the pictures with the twins at bedtime."

"Good night," said the twins.

"Good night," said a little voice under the blankets; and in no time, Robert was asleep.

2
Robert's book

"There they are, Robert!" called out Mrs. Price as first there was a ring at the door-bell, and then a loud rat-a-tat. "All that noise could only be the twins!"

Robert dashed to the front door. He'd been waiting impatiently all afternoon for Joanna and Stephen to come home from school. He couldn't reach the lock on the front door, though, so he had to wait for Mrs. Price to come and open it.

"Hallo, Robert," said Joanna, as she hung her satchel on a peg in the hall. "Have you had a good time playing with our toys?"

Robert nodded his head vigorously.

"Yes, he has," said Mrs. Price. "He had Stephen's trains out this morning."

"Not my electric ones?" said Stephen anxiously, thinking that Robert was far too young to play with electric trains on his own.

"Oh, no," answered his mother. "We found your old clockwork train and the rails. Then he played with your fort and Joanna's dolls house."

"Better than going to school!" exclaimed Stephen.

"And he helped me hang out the washing," went on Mrs. Price. "But how about you two? I expect you're hungry. What did you have for dinner to-day?"

"Sausages again," said Joanna, "and treacle tart afterwards, but it was all pastry."

"Tea's ready on the table. Robert opposite me, and you two either side."

Joanna remembered her mother's promise of last night. "Did Mummy buy you a Bible colouring book, Robert?"

"Mmmm, do you want to see it?"

Before Joanna could answer, her mother said, "Not now, Jo. It's tea-time, and we don't have books at the table. After tea you can see it, and later on we can talk about the pictures with Robert."

*   *   *

Robert turned over the first pages of his colouring book.

"I did three pictures today—look!"

Stephen looked closely and rather critically at one of the pictures. "You didn't keep in the lines very well there."

"Nor did you when you were four!" interrupted his mother from the kitchen, where she was putting away the crockery.

"Look," said Joanna, trying to make up for Stephen's comment, "he did that one nicely."

The picture was of the stable at Bethlehem. Mary

and Joseph were on the right of the picture, and in Mary's lap was the baby Jesus, while next to her was the manger He was to be laid in. On the left of the picture there were three shepherds.

Mrs. Price came and sat down with them.

"Tell us who all the people are, Robert," she suggested.

"That's Mary in blue; and Joseph standing next to her."

"Who are the people visiting them?"

"The shepherds."

Across the top of the picture there was the word EMMANUEL to be coloured in, and underneath in small letters the words 'God with us'. Robert had coloured EMMANUEL in with red and the words underneath in yellow.

"Mummy," Stephen asked. "Why has it got under EMMANUEL the words 'God with us'?"

"Because that's what the word 'Emmanuel' means. You'll find it in the first chapter in St. Matthew's Gospel. Run upstairs and get your Bible and you can see."

In half a minute Stephen was back, having found chapter one on his way downstairs. "I've found it," he said. "Verses twenty-two and twenty-three: 'All this took place to fulfil what the Lord had spoken by the prophet: Behold, a virgin shall conceive, and bear a son, and his name shall be called Emmanuel (which means God with us).' "

Mrs. Price nodded. "If you look in the margin,

you'll see it says that the prophet Isaiah said this would happen."

"Did the prophets know all about Jesus coming, Mummy?" asked Joanna.

"Yes; they were like look-out men. They wanted to tell God's people when the Messiah, the Christ, was going to come. They knew that He would be more than just a man. They spoke of Him as being both God and man."

Stephen believed that Jesus was a man, and that He is God too, but he didn't understand it very well. "How do we know that Jesus is God and man, Mum? It happened such a long time ago, didn't it?"

"Well," began Mrs. Price thoughtfully, "you've just read what the prophet Isaiah said, that Jesus would be 'God with us'. I can remember a verse in Micah, too. May I have your Bible a moment, please, Steve?"

Mrs. Price turned the pages over.

"I'm glad you didn't ask me to find Micah, Mum," said Stephen with relief. "I get lost in those books at the end of the Old Testament."

His mother smiled. "Look, here it is. Micah, chapter five, verse two. You read it to us, Steve."

" 'But you, O Bethlehem Ephrathah, who are little to be among the clans of Judah, from you shall come forth for me one who is to be ruler in Israel; whose origin is from of old, from ancient days.' "

"Well read," congratulated his mother. "Now, only God has always existed. But Micah said that the Christ who was going to be born as a human baby in Bethlehem had always existed. So he knew that Christ would be both God and man."

"Was Jesus a kind of superman?" asked Stephen, remembering the stories in his comics.

"Definitely not," replied Mrs. Price. "He was really a man, and He was really God—at the same time. The Bible doesn't explain this because it's too difficult for us to understand. But it tells us that it is true. The disciples knew it was. Jesus was a man all right; they met Him just as they met anyone else, and they got to know Him well. Then they discovered that He was God. Everything they saw about Jesus made them know that He was God's Son."

Joanna had been thinking about Robert's picture. "Is that why His birth was different? Joseph wasn't really Jesus' father, was he?"

"No," agreed Mrs. Price. "Do you remember I told you how you came to be born?"

"Yes," Joanna nodded.

"Good," Mrs. Price went on. "Well Jesus' human life began inside Mary by a miracle performed by the Holy Spirit, so that Jesus had no human father, only a human mother."

"And it wasn't make-believe, was it?" Stephen remembered how once he had had to pretend he was an angel in a nativity play at school. "Jesus didn't kind of dress up as a man?"

"Oh, no, He grew up as a boy, like you. Look at Robert's picture."

Robert hadn't been able to understand what the twins and Mrs. Price were talking about, and had started colouring the fourth picture in the book. It was a drawing of Jesus in the temple in Jerusalem, asking questions.

Mrs. Price went on, "When He was a boy, Jesus liked asking questions, just as you do. He was sometimes tired, and thirsty. He was like us in every way, except for one thing. Do you know what that was?"

Joanna answered first. "Jesus never sinned."

"There must have been a very important reason for Jesus to become a man," Stephen had been thinking hard.

"Yes," agreed his mother, "only someone who was perfect could die in the place of sinners to pay the price of their sin. And there wasn't a single man good enough to do it. You know why, don't you? Jo hinted at it just now."

"Because everyone's sinned," answered Stephen.

"But how do you know that everyone everywhere has sinned?" asked Joanna.

Her mother smiled. "First of all, the Bible tells us so. And then we know we have sinned. You have, haven't you?"

Stephen and Joanna nodded.

"What about you, Robert? Have you ever been naughty and not done what Mummy and Daddy told you?"

Robert looked at the floor and scuffed his feet.

"Oh, don't look so miserable!" Mrs. Price said

with a laugh. "I'm not going to tell you off! But you see, our sin shows how much we need a Saviour. Being God and being a perfect man, Jesus was able to die for sinners, so that they could be forgiven."

Robert had finished the picture of Jesus in the temple now. It was by far the best he had done.

"You've coloured that very well, Robert," congratulated Mrs. Price.

Joanna looked at Stephen. "Let's play a game with Robert."

"O.K.; what shall we play?"

"I spy with my little eye."

"All right. Can you play that, Robert?"

Robert shook his head and looked as if he was about to burst into tears.

"I don't expect he can spell yet," whispered Mrs. Price to Joanna.

"Sorry," Joanna apologised. "But we can play it with colours instead. I spy with my little eye something—bright red!"

And since the only bright red thing in the room was Robert's pullover, he guessed it straightaway, and insisted on playing I spy right up till bedtime.

3

Postcards from Scotland

"The postman's coming down the road," exclaimed Joanna, as the Price family and young Robert sat eating their breakfast.

"I don't expect he'll come here."

"He may have some bills for Daddy, though, Steve," said Mrs. Price.

Mr. Price made a face. "He can keep those!"

"He only brings things for me on my birthday and at Christmas."

"You never know, Robert," Mrs. Price said, "your Mummy and Daddy may write to you."

Joanna had kept her eyes on the window. "He *is* coming here. Can I go and get the post, please?"

"Whose turn is it?" asked her father.

"It's mine."

"All right."

Joanna ran to the door just as the postman slipped the post through the letter box. There was a letter addressed to Mr. and Mrs. Price, and two postcards, one addressed to Robert and the other to the twins.

"They've all got the same postmark, Daddy."

Mr. Price looked at the postmark on the letter.

"It's from Robert's parents. Your card looks exciting, Robert."

"It's a Scottish soldier, and he's playing the bagpipes. But I can't read what the card says."

Joanna was sitting next to Robert, so she read the card. "We shall not be away long now. Lots of love, Mummy and Daddy."

Mr. Price had been reading Mr. and Mrs. Fyson's letter. He passed it to his wife, and said, "The funeral of Mr. Fyson's mother is on Thursday. They hope to come back on Saturday."

Robert was listening to what Mr. Price said. He didn't understand what a 'funeral' was, though he knew his grandmother had died.

*   *   *

In the afternoon Robert went out shopping with Mrs. Price. Afterwards they went to meet Stephen and Joanna from school. The roads were very busy, and at the biggest crossroads there was a man wearing a white coat. He had a long pole with a notice on top.

"Do you know what the twins used to call that man when they were little, Robert?"

"No, what?"

"They used to call him the lollipop man! That notice on the end of the pole looks rather like a lollipop, doesn't it?"

"Can I have a lollipop?"

Mrs. Price laughed. "All right. We'll go into the sweet shop and you can choose one for yourself and one for each of the twins."

As they came out of the sweet shop four large black cars drove slowly past. Robert liked cars, and he collected model ones.

"Is that a wedding?" he asked.

"Oh, no! It's a funeral."

"Like Granny will have on Thursday?"

"Yes; just like that."

"What are all the flowers for?"

"All the people who knew and loved the person who died, want to show their love by sending flowers," explained Mrs. Price.

"Can I send some to Granny's?"

"Yes, you can, Robert. That would be kind. Uncle's going to arrange for some to be sent from us all. He'll put your name on the card that goes with them."

By the time all Robert's questions had been answered, they were at the school, just in time to catch Stephen and Joanna as they came out of the school gates.

When they arrived home, Mrs. Price said, "Well, what have you decided to do with Robert this evening?"

"Colouring, Mummy," said Joanna.

"We want to make our own pictures," Stephen added. "Then you can judge them. It'll be a kind of competition."

"That's not fair, you can draw better than me," Robert said.

"You can colour one of the pictures in your Bible colouring book, then," suggested Stephen.

Mrs. Price thought this was a good idea too.

Robert's picture was a very gay one. There was a crowded street with lots of men in a sort of procession. On one side there was Jesus and His disciples. Next to Him was a woman with her arms round someone who looked as if he was her son. There were words to be coloured at the top of the picture—'Jesus went about doing good'. The title for the picture was at the bottom of the page—'The Widow of Nain'.

"Shall I tell you the story, Robert?" Mrs. Price suggested.

"Yes, please," replied Robert eagerly.

"Jesus went to a town called Nain. His disciples were with Him, and lots of other people. As Jesus came up to the gate of the town, He met a funeral. It wouldn't have been like the one we saw this afternoon; there were no cars then. And I don't expect they sent flowers as we do. Men would carry the dead person on a kind of stretcher—like you see ambulance men using. Lots of people would follow these men to the place where the person was buried. Now this dead man was his mother's only son. He meant a lot to her because her husband had died not long before and he was the only family she had. When the Lord Jesus saw her, He was very sorry for her. He knew how much she would miss her son. He said to her, 'Don't cry any more.' Then He stepped forward and laid His hand on the stretcher. The men carrying it stopped. Then Jesus said, 'Young man, rise up!' Then do you know what happened?"

"Did he get up?" Robert asked in amazement.

"Yes; he sat up and began to talk; and Jesus gave him back to his mother. And wasn't she happy and thankful to Jesus!"

Robert looked thoughtful. "Why didn't Jesus make Granny better?"

"I don't know, Robert," replied Mrs. Price. "Jesus doesn't tell us the answers to questions like that now. I expect it was because she was very old. We needn't be sorry for her. She loved Jesus, didn't she?"

Robert nodded.

"Then it's better for her to be with Jesus in heaven. If she had got better, she would still have been weak and old. But with Jesus she is in the most exciting place anywhere. We don't have to be afraid of dying when we love and trust the Lord Jesus."

Joanna and Stephen had been listening. They were both sitting at the table, drawing and colouring. Stephen had started drawing his own picture of the widow of Nain's son being healed.

"Did Jesus heal everyone?"

"No, He didn't, Steve. Usually He only healed the people who came to Him. It was unusual for Him to do what He did in Nain, without being asked.

But He healed all kinds of diseases and illnesses, didn't He? Let's see, how many can you think of?"

"The blind and the deaf."

"And the dumb and the lame."

"The paralysed man."

"Lepers."

"That's six, anyway," Mrs. Price added them up. "And there were many others too."

"Why didn't Jesus heal everyone?" asked Stephen, puzzled.

"One reason was that He couldn't be everywhere at once and He didn't only come to heal people. You see," Mrs. Price explained, "He came to teach the people about God and what God wanted them to know."

"But didn't people need to be healed more than taught, Mummy?"

"No, not really, Stephen. They may have thought so. But their souls—the invisible part of us that lives for ever—are more important. I know a story that will help you to understand. Can you fetch me Daddy's new Bible, please—and I'll read it to you."

Stephen went over to the book-case.

"Can I read it, Mummy?"

"All right, Jo. Mark, chapter two, verses one to twelve."

So Joanna read: "When after some days he returned to Capernaum, the news went round that he was at home; and such a crowd collected that the space in front of the door was not big enough to hold them. And while he was proclaiming the message to them, a man was brought who was paralysed. Four men were carrying him, but because of the crowd they could not get him near. So they opened up the roof over the place where Jesus was, and when they had broken through they lowered the stretcher on which the paralysed man was lying. When Jesus saw their faith, he said to the paralysed man, 'My son, your sins are forgiven.' Now there were some lawyers sitting there and they thought to themselves, 'Why does the fellow talk like that? This is blasphemy! Who but God alone can forgive sins?' Jesus knew in his own mind that this was what they were thinking, and said to them: 'Why do you harbour thoughts like these? Is it easier to say to this paralysed man, "Your sins are forgiven" or to say "Stand up, take your bed, and walk"? But to convince you that the Son of Man has the right on earth to forgive sins'—he turned to the paralysed man—'I say to you, stand up, take your bed, and go home.' And he got up, took his stretcher at once, and went out in full view of them all, so that they were astounded and praised God. 'Never before,' they said, 'have we seen the like.' "

"Good,' commented Mrs. Price at the end. "Now, what was wrong with the man?"

"He was paralysed," answered Stephen.

"Do you know what that means, Robert?"

Robert shook his head.

Mrs. Price explained. "He couldn't walk or move

on his own. He was crippled. Now, Jo, what did Jesus say first of all to the paralysed man? Did He tell him to stand up straight away?"

'No, Mum," Joanna ran her finger down the story. "He told him that his sins were forgiven. Then, afterwards, He told him to get up."

"That's right. Jesus did this to teach us that it's more important to have our sins forgiven than to have our bodies healed. Jesus knew that His first task was to teach God's Word. He cared too, of course, for people's bodies. But He knew that our bodies die, but our souls live for ever. If people believed His words, and obeyed them, their sins would be forgiven by God."

Joanna nodded. "You told us yesterday that Jesus was really God and man. How do we know that Jesus is God?"

"That's a big question," Stephen said.

"Yes," agreed Mrs. Price. She picked up Robert's colouring book. "The next picture is Jesus turning water into wine. That was one of the miracles which showed who He was. Leave that picture till tomorrow, Robert; and then we'll get Joanna's Daddy to answer her question. Now then, let me see all these beautiful pictures of yours!"

4
Mr. Price joins in

Mrs. Price was washing up after dinner. For most of the morning Robert had played with Stephen's soldiers and cars. But after dinner he got bored, and didn't know what to do. Mrs. Price suggested he should colour the next picture in his book. It was the picture of Jesus at the wedding in Cana, where He turned the water into wine. As a treat she let him use Joanna's paints; it made a change from ordinary colouring pencils.

When she'd finished tidying up in the kitchen, she put her head round the door. "Have you finished the picture yet, Robert?"

"Yes. But I've made a mess with the water. I knocked some over."

Mrs. Price smiled. She remembered Stephen and Joanna doing the same when they were Robert's age. She had put plenty of newspaper on the table, so it didn't matter.

"Never mind," she said. "But tidy up now, and put the painting on the sideboard to dry. The twins will want to see it."

"What can I do now?"

"Wait a few minutes and I'll come and play a game with you."

Mrs. Price had been washing up some of the milk bottles ready to put out on the front step for the milkman. It reminded her of a game Mr. Price had shown the twins last holidays. All she needed was one of the milk bottles and a box of matches.

"Look, Robert," she explained. "I'll put this bottle on the floor between us. Now we take it in turns to put a match on top of the bottle. We want to get as many as we can on top without knocking one off. If you knock one off, you lose the game."

Robert thought it was easy. And it was at first; but the more matches they balanced on the mouth of the milk bottle, the more difficult it became. Once Mrs. Price knocked two off and Robert won. And several times Robert knocked them off.

"This is fun," exclaimed Robert. "Can I play this with Stephen and Joanna?"

They became so clever at the game that they used up a whole box of matches without knocking one off.

"What do we do now? Have we both won?"

"No," explained Mrs. Price. "We have to take them off one by one. If you knock them down or take more than one off, you lose."

Very carefully they took them off. But it was not long before Mrs. Price knocked three off at once.

"You've won, Robert. Now, tell me what you'd like for tea today."

"Oh, peanut butter, please! Not the crunchy sort, the smooth."

Mrs. Price went to the larder. "Oh, dear, I'm afraid there isn't any left, Robert."

Robert looked disappointed, and Mrs. Price wished she hadn't asked him what he would like.

"Could we buy some when we go and meet the twins?"

Mrs. Price thought for a moment. "Well, I wasn't going to meet them today. And it's Wednesday anyway—the shops are closed."

Suddenly the telephone rang. Robert soon guessed that Mrs. Price was talking to her husband. After she had listened to what Mr. Price had to say, she said, "And could you call in at the shops for me on your way home? I want some peanut better for tea. Oh, yes, the smooth kind, please. 'Bye."

Mrs. Price looked at Robert. "Well, Robert, that's fine! Mr. Price is coming home early. He's going to meet the twins from school as a surprise, and he'll get the peanut butter before he meets them. The shops near his office close on Thursdays."

*   *   *

Sharp at ten past four the twins arrived home.

"Daddy met us, Mum!" they shouted.

"Yes; that was a surprise for you. And it's lovely to have Daddy home so early for a change."

One of the first things they saw as they came into the dining-room was Robert's picture on the sideboard, where he had left it to dry.

"That's a good picture, Robert," commented Mr. Price.

"You're going to talk to us about it," explained Joanna.

"Am I?" asked Mr. Price in surprise.

"Yes, Dad," confirmed Stephen. "We were talking to Mummy last night about it; we asked her how we know that Jesus is God."

Joanna joined in. "Mummy said that the turning of water into wine was one of the miracles which showed who Jesus was."

"Yes, that's right," agreed Mr. Price. "Do you know the story, Robert?"

"Not really."

"Stephen and Joanna, you tell the story first, then."

"There was a wedding in a place called Cana," Stephen began. "And Jesus was invited to the wedding."

"And some of His disciples too," added Joanna.

"Yes, and Mary, Jesus' mother, was there. They ran out of wine at this wedding. So Mary went to Jesus and told Him. I think she expected Him to send one of His disciples to buy some."

"Like Mummy running out of peanut butter and asking me to get some, Robert!" put in Mr. Price with a grin.

They all laughed.

"Go on, Steve."

"Before Mary went back to the wedding feast, she said to the servants, 'Do whatever Jesus tells you to.' Now, standing against the wall there were some stone water-pots—I forget how many."

"Wait a moment, then," said Mr. Price. "You can see them in Robert's picture. You count them, Robert."

"One, two, three, four, five, six. Six water-pots!" shouted Robert.

"What happened then, Jo?" Mr. Price asked.

"Jesus told the servants to fill the water-pots with water right up to the brim. Then He told them to take some of it out of the water-pots and carry it into the feast. And they did as He told them."

"What happened to the water, Robert, do you think?" enquired Mr. Price.

"Had it turned to wine?"

"Yes; into the very best wine. Finish the story, Jo."

"The servants took the water into the feast, and the people tasted it. The man in charge of the feast was surprised. It was the best wine he had ever tasted. So he said to the bridegroom 'When people have a party, they always give the best wine first, and the poor wine last. But you've kept the best until last.' Not one of the guests knew how it had happened. But the servants and Jesus' disciples knew."

"That's a wonderful story," said Mr. Price when Joanna finished. "Jesus did what no one else could do. He could command something to happen, and it happened."

Stephen remembered the story of creation he had heard at Sunday School on Harvest Sunday. "When God made everything, He just spoke and it happened like that, too, didn't it, Daddy?"

"Yes. Just the same, Steve. Jesus showed He could do what only God can do. All the miracles showed this. He didn't do them for Himself, but always to help others and to show them who He was. People were amazed at His power—just as they were at the wedding when they found water made into wine."

"People were surprised at His teaching too, weren't they, Daddy?" Joanna thought she remembered reading this in the Bible.

"True. Do you know what happened once when some soldiers were sent to arrest Jesus?"

"No."

"The soldiers found where Jesus was and went to arrest Him. But there was such a large crowd they couldn't easily get to Him. So they had to listen, while they waited for the crowd to go home. But as they heard Him speaking, they thought His words were very special; they had never heard such teaching! They felt they couldn't arrest such a good person, so they went back without Jesus! They got into trouble for it too. 'But,' they said, 'we never heard anyone teach like this before.' Things like this all showed that Jesus is God."

Stephen asked, "Did Jesus say He was God, Daddy?"

"Yes, He did," replied Mr. Price. "But not very often. Instead He said and did things which only God can say and do. There were times when He said and admitted that He was the Messiah the Jews were waiting for. This was the same as saying that He is God, because the Jews knew the Messiah would have a very special relationship to God. Jesus also said things about Himself that no ordinary man would say, except perhaps an imposter."

"What's an imposter, Dad?"

"Do you know, Steve?"

"Someone who pretends to be someone else, isn't it?"

"Yes," went on Mr. Price. "Jesus said some things

that we wouldn't dare say. Supposing, Steve, you said, 'I'm the best footballer in the world'. What would people say?"

"They would say I was big-headed and boasting, and it wasn't true!"

"Well, Jesus said things—far more important than playing football—and there was nothing boastful about it. He told His disciples that He is the Way, the Truth and the Life, and that no one can come to God the Father without first coming to Him. These were big things to say. But they are true."

Joanna remembered something her mother had said. "When we were talking to Mum, she told us that Jesus was like us in everything except for one thing—he never sinned."

"That's right. This is another proof that Jesus is God. He never disobeyed His Father. He was never deceitful or selfish."

"How do we know for sure, Daddy?" asked Stephen.

"The disciples who lived with Jesus said so. When we live with someone, we really know what he is like. I remember someone once saying when we were out that you looked 'angelic'. It was when you were much smaller! But I had to say that you weren't always 'angelic' at home!"

"He isn't now either, Daddy!"

"Neither are you, Jo! But the disciples lived with Jesus and knew what Jesus was like. And they wrote it down in the Bible lots of times. They would have known if He wasn't really good. So we can be sure that Jesus is God."

He paused and thought for a moment. "Is there a picture of the Resurrection of Jesus in your book, Robert?"

Robert didn't know.

"I'll look for you, Robert," Stephen offered. "Yes, there is—here!"

"Good. When you come to that, I'll tell you how the Resurrection shows that Jesus is God. But that's enough for now."

Robert had been dying to say something and finally succeeded in getting everyone's attention. "Can we play a game?"

"Yes, all right. What would you like?"

"Seeing how many matchsticks we can put on top of a milk bottle!"

Stephen and Joanna looked surprised. "Do you know how to play that, Robert?"

"Your Mummy showed me this afternoon. I'm ever so good at it!"

"We'll soon see about that!" said Mr. Price, winking at the twins.

And by the time Robert had to go to bed, Stephen had won three times, Joanna and Robert four times each, and Mr. Price eleven times—but the others said that was because he made them laugh just when it was getting difficult, which wasn't fair.

5
Mr Price brings home a surprise

It was blowing half a gale as the twins walked home from school with their mother and Robert.

"Daddy's been on the phone," Mrs. Price told the twins. "He's got a surprise for you."

"What is it, Mummy?" Stephen and Joanna asked together.

"Now, now! It wouldn't be a surprise if I told you, would it? Wait and see!"

"Oh, go on, give us a clue!"

Mrs. Price smiled. "Well, you remember the book token he had for his birthday?"

"Yes."

"He went into that big bookshop at lunch time. He really meant to buy himself a book. But he saw a new children's book—but you'll have to wait and see what it is!"

"Is it for both of us?" asked Stephen.

"Yes, Steve. It's a book to share, and Daddy will work out how you share it."

Robert had heard about the book from Mrs. Price after Mr. Price had rung her up earlier on, so he wasn't interested now. He was busy watching everything they passed.

"What's that?"

"What's what, Robert?" asked Stephen.

Robert pointed to a large cross in the garden in front of a church. On the cross there was a figure of a man. The cross was made of wood, and the man was made of metal.

"That's meant to be like the cross Jesus died on," explained Stephen. "It's a kind of statue of Jesus."

Robert looked puzzled, but he didn't ask any more questions.

*   *   *

Without telling each other, Stephen and Joanna were both listening for the sound of their father's car stopping outside. At twenty past five came the familiar noise.

"There's Daddy's car!"

They both rushed to the front door as their father came in.

"Where is it, Daddy?"

"Where's what?" replied Mr. Price, pretending to be surprised.

"The book!"

"What book?" questioned Mr. Price, as if he didn't know what they were talking about.

"Daddy, you are a tease!" shouted Joanna.

"All right," laughed Mr. Price. "After tea I'll show

it to you. But tea first, because I'm sure Mummy's got it ready for us."

*   *   *

About a quarter of an hour later, Mrs. Price exclaimed, "That's the fastest tea you children have eaten for a long time!"

"We want to see the new book, Mummy," Joanna explained.

Mr. Price sat down on the settee; Stephen and Joanna sat either side, and Robert stood in between Mr. Price and Stephen. Carefully Mr. Price unwrapped his big parcel. It was a lovely, brightly coloured book of Bible stories, with pictures on every page.

"Ooooh!" said all the children in chorus.

"Which picture would you like to see first?"

"Jonah and the whale," Joanna managed to say first.

There were four pictures about Jonah. There was one of Jonah going into the ship, then one of the ship at sea in a tremendous storm. The picture of Jonah washed up on the shore after being in the big fish took up nearly two whole pages. The last picture was of the huge tree which Jonah had sat under when he sulked.

"What now, Dad?" Stephen asked.

"Let Robert choose."

"Jesus on the cross, please."

Mr. Price turned the pages until he found the place. The picture took up almost two pages. On one page there were three crosses, with Jesus hanging on the one in the middle. On the other page there were the soldiers. They had taken Jesus' coat, and they were throwing dice to see who should have it.

"It reminds me of 'There is a green hill', Daddy."

"Yes, Jo. If Robert knows it, we could sing the first verse together."

"Yes, I do," nodded Robert.

And so they sang the first verse:

> 'There is a green hill far away,
> Without a city wall,
> Where the dear Lord was crucified
> Who died to save us all.'

"Weren't the soldiers cruel and unkind," Joanna said as she looked at the picture.

Mr. Price agreed. "But I expect if Jesus had lived on earth nowadays, people would have treated Him in more or less the same way."

"Do you think Jesus knew when He was a boy that He would have to die on the cross?" she asked.

"The Bible doesn't tell us much about that," answered Mr. Price. "But Jesus knew before He first met Peter and John and all the other disciples. Once Jesus asked the disciples, 'Who do men say that I am?' The disciples told Him that some thought He was John the Baptist, others Elijah, others Jeremiah or one of the prophets. And then Jesus asked, 'Who do you say I am?' And Peter said, 'You are the Christ, the Son of the living God.' "

"I remember," Joanna butted in, "didn't Jesus tell them then that He was going to die?"

Mr. Price nodded. "Yes. He told His disciples that He must go to Jerusalem, and that He would suffer a lot there because wicked men would put Him to death. When Peter heard this he was very angry, and Jesus had to tell him off."

"But when did Jesus first know that He had to die?" persisted Joanna.

"When He was very young, I expect," suggested Stephen. "But He couldn't have known when He was a little baby, could He, Dad? Babies don't know or understand difficult things."

Mrs. Price had come into the room and heard what

Stephen said. "You do ask Daddy difficult questions!"

"You can help me answer them, dear."

"Well," said Mrs. Price. "I'm sure Jesus knew when He was a little boy that He was God's Son and that He was going to die on the cross when He was older. But the Bible doesn't tell us when He first knew this. You mustn't forget that Jesus didn't begin His life when He was born into this world: He is God, and lives for ever. He came into the world purposely to die on the cross for us."

"Was Jesus an ordinary baby like Sarah across the road?" asked Joanna. "Did He cry and grow like other children?"

"Yes, I'm sure He did. But although He was like other babies to look at, He was different because He was not only human, He was God as well. As He grew up, He knew He was God's Son. We talked about this a little the other day."

"When, Mummy?"

"When I told you about Jesus going to Jerusalem, Steve. Jesus wasn't very much older than you are now. He went up to Jerusalem for the special services the Jews had in the temple. Mary and Joseph took Him with them. When the feast was over, Mary and Joseph started back home, but Jesus stayed in Jerusalem because He wanted to spend more time in the temple. Mary and Joseph didn't know that Jesus wasn't with them; they thought He was playing with friends in some other part of the crowd going home from Jerusalem. They walked for a whole day without seeing Him. Then they began to look for Him among their friends and relations."

"I remember," said Joanna. "When they couldn't find Him they went back to Jerusalem to look for Him. They looked for three whole days before they found Him sitting in the temple with the teachers, listening to them and asking questions."

"That's right. And everyone who heard Jesus was surprised at His intelligence and the answers He gave. Mary and Joseph were cross with Jesus because of the trouble they had had finding Him. Do you remember what He said?"

"Yes. He said 'Didn't you know that I must be about My Father's business?' " Then Stephen understood why his mother had mentioned Jesus' visit to the temple. "I see now. Jesus knew at least when He was twelve that He was the Son of God, and if He knew that, He must have known too that He had come into the world to die for our sins."

"I should think so," his mother agreed. "As Jesus' body grew, so did His knowledge of who He was and why He had come. No one had to tell Jesus that He was God's Son and why He had come; He knew without anyone telling Him."

Joanna was thoughtful. "If Jesus knew from the time He was a little boy that He was going to die on the cross, He must have been brave."

"Yes. And He must love us very much too, Jo."

"That picture's in my book," interrupted Robert.

"What picture, Robert?" asked Mrs. Price.

"Jesus in the temple."

"So it is. You coloured it, didn't you?"

But Robert was looking at the other picture, in the book Mr. Price had brought home—the picture of Jesus dying on the cross. "Jesus is still on the cross, isn't He?" he asked.

"Oh, no, dear," replied Mrs. Price.

"He is, I know."

"What do you mean, Robert?"

"I saw Him."

"When?"

"Outside that church."

Then Mrs. Price understood. "That was only a kind of statue, Robert. Jesus didn't stay on the cross. They took Him down when they were sure that He had died. But He didn't stay dead. Three days later He came back to life again. And hundreds of people saw Him. And He's alive today. When you see the cross with the man on it again, you remember that Jesus didn't stay on the cross; He's alive. Right now, time for bed, Robert!"

"Oh, no, not yet, please! Can't we play with the matches and the milk bottle again?"

"Let's!" shouted the twins.

"Just ten minutes, then."

And without Mr. Price to make them giggle, Joanna won twice as many times as anyone else which, she said, just went to prove that girls were better at everything.

6
Marbles

"What are these?" Robert lifted a small plastic bag from a shelf of the book-case in the dining-room.

Mrs. Price came across and looked. "Oh, they're marbles."

"What are marbles?"

"They're little balls of glass and you play a game with them."

"Are they Stephen's?"

"Well, really, Robert, they're Mr. Price's! Last Christmas he was given them from the Christmas tree. He didn't open the bag because we had a little baby staying with us, and she crawled all over the floor. He didn't want her to play with them and per-haps put one in her mouth and swallow it. So he put them in the book-case. The twins forgot all about them, I suppose."

"Can we play with them?"

Mrs. Price smiled. She hadn't played marbles for years and years, and could hardly remember how to play.

"All right. Let's count them out."

There were twenty marbles; so Robert and Mrs. Price had ten each.

"Now I'll start by rolling one of mine along the carpet. Then you have to try and roll one of your marbles to hit it. If you hit it, then you win my marble. If you miss, I can try to hit your marble. Every time you hit the other person's marble, then it belongs to you. Ready?"

"Yes," replied Robert eagerly.

Time flew, and Robert became very good at hitting Mrs. Price's marbles. Mrs. Price's knees began to ache from kneeling, and Robert started rolling his marbles so hard that they often went under the sideboard. Mrs. Price had to get a long knitting needle to poke them out from underneath.

Suddenly they heard the back door open.

"Is that Stephen and Joanna already?" Mrs. Price exclaimed.

The dining-room door opened and the twins burst in.

"What are you doing on the floor, Mum?"

"We're playing marbles, Jo," Mrs. Price said from underneath the table. "We found the packet Daddy had last Christmas from the Christmas tree. Robert discovered them in the book-case."

"I wondered where they'd gone," Stephen said. "Can we have a game?"

"You'd better ask Robert, Steve. He's won all my marbles except this one!"

Robert was keen to play again, so Stephen helped him count out the marbles.

"Joanna can play with me first, if she likes," Robert offered.

"All right," agreed Stephen.

Mrs. Price began to lay the table for tea.

"What kind of day have you two had at school?"

"Oh, good and bad, Mum," answered Stephen.

"Why was that?"

"Well," Stephen went on to explain, "it was good because I've been given a place in the football team. I didn't think I was going to get a game, even though I've been first reserve all term. But Malcolm has to go away this week-end, so he can't play on Satur-

day. Mr. Trench said I'm to play instead. I do hope
I play well."

"You can only do your best, Steve. Daddy will be
pleased. What was bad about today?"

"It was Michael Rogers."

"What about him?"

"Mrs. Foxleigh went out of the room—to get new
exercise books, I think. Michael threw a conker
across the room. I think he was trying to hit Ian.
But the conker rolled right out to the front. Everyone was laughing and making a racket."

"You and Jo as well?"

Stephen nodded. "But that wasn't the bad bit.
John Foster knew that Mrs. Foxleigh would see the
conker as soon as she came back, and he didn't want
Michael to get into trouble. So he went out to the
front to get it. Just as he was picking it up—and
everyone was talking—Mrs. Foxleigh came in. She
was ever so cross. She thought he'd caused all the
trouble, so she made him stay in after school and
help her tidy up."

"Didn't he tell Mrs. Foxleigh the truth?"

"Oh, no, Michael's his friend. Michael knew he
ought to get into trouble. But John shook his head
when Michael put up his hand to own up. It was
decent of John to do that for Michael, wasn't it?"

Mrs. Price agreed. "When Daddy was talking
about the cross last night, I wondered how we could
help you understand what happened. But I think I
can explain now."

"How, Mum?" Stephen enquired.

"When Jesus died on the cross, He didn't deserve to die. He had never sinned or done anything wrong. But He died in our place, to pay the price of sin. He was our substitute. He took our place, just as Steve will be taking Malcolm's place on Saturday. Malcolm ought to play, but Steve will play instead. We ought to be punished for our sins, but Jesus died in our place."

"Were you thinking of John Foster, too?" asked Joanna.

"Yes. Michael did wrong. But John took the punishment. We did wrong; but Jesus took our punishment on the cross."

*   *   *

After tea Joanna was sitting on the settee next to her father, turning over the pages of the new Bible picture book.

"Look, Daddy, there's a picture of the Resurrection. Aren't you going to tell us about it? You promised to tell us how the Resurrection shows that Jesus is God."

"Yes, but I said when Robert got that far in his painting book."

Mrs. Price interrupted. "That will be never then, I'm afraid! We had an accident; all the paints were spilt over the book! So we decided to throw it away."

Robert looked ashamed. "I'm sorry," he said in a small voice.

"That doesn't matter, Robert. Come and stand by me and see this picture of the Resurrection. Look, there are the women who went early to the tomb. But when they got there, they found it was empty. And look, here's another picture. There's Jesus in the middle of the room, with the disciples standing round Him. They were all there, except Thomas. The Resurrection was like God saying to everyone, 'Jesus is my Son.'"

"What do you mean, Daddy?" Joanna asked, puzzled.

"Well, let me ask you some questions. Did Jesus let people know that He was God before He died?"

Joanna nodded.

"Did Jesus really die when He was put on the cross?"

"Yes, Daddy."

"Could any man or woman have given Him life again?"

"Of course not."

"Who raised Him from the dead, then?"

"God did."

"Would God have raised Jesus from the dead if Jesus hadn't spoken the truth when He said He was the Son of God?"

"No, I suppose He wouldn't have."

"Well, when God raised Jesus from the dead He was letting everyone know that Jesus is His Son.

You imagine a boy at school telling you that his Daddy was very important. How would you know if it was true?"

Joanna thought for a moment. "By seeing him with the man, and hearing him speak to him?"

"I see what you mean, Dad," interrupted Stephen. "Last term one of the boys told us that his father was a high-up in the Navy. We didn't believe him. But then one day an officer was waiting outside school. We could tell he was important by his uniform. This boy ran straight out of school to meet him, and I heard the officer say, 'Hello, son.' I knew then that he'd told the truth, and I told the others."

"Fine, Steve," said Mr. Price. "Well, in the same way, the Resurrection was God saying to everyone, 'Jesus is my Son.' Jesus appeared to the women, to Peter and to the disciples. At one time He appeared to more than five hundred believers together. God wanted them all to be sure that Jesus is His Son. And then God made certain that it was all written down in the Bible so that people like us could be sure too."

Robert had gone to the bottom shelf of the bookcase again to fetch the marbles; he'd given up trying to follow what the others were saying a long time ago.

"Look what I found this afternoon!"

"My marbles!" exclaimed Mr. Price. He pretended to be cross. "Who's been playing with them?"

"I have—with Auntie and Joanna."

Mr. Price smiled. "Have you played yet, Steve?"

"Not yet, Dad."

"I'll play you, then!"

Stephen and Mr. Price played far more violently than Robert and Joanna, and soon there were marbles all over the place. Finally Mrs. Price came in. "Dear me!" she said. "What a noise! I really think it's time for the three boys to go to bed now," and she winked at Joanna.

7
Robert's last day

Robert was sharing Stephen's bedroom. On Saturday morning he woke up first, and thought he'd wake Stephen.

"Stephen. Wake up! It's Saturday morning!"

Stephen grunted, rolled over and finally sat up, not really sorry that Robert had woken him up.

"Jolly good. No school today, and Daddy doesn't have to go to work. So we can do lots of things today."

"Yes," agreed Robert, "but I didn't meant that. My Mummy and Daddy are coming home today!"

"Oh, yes, I'd forgotten all about that, Robert! It will seem funny not having you share my room."

* * *

On Saturday mornings breakfast was later, and it was half past nine before Stephen had eaten his last piece of toast and marmalade.

"Are you excited, Robert?" asked Joanna, as Robert was finishing his cornflakes.

"Mmm," nodded Robert. Then after a moment

he said, "I didn't want to talk with my mouth full.
I didn't want to be a Goop."

Mr. Price laughed. "Have they taught you that,
Robert? Can you say the words on your own?"

Robert was keen to show Mr. Price that he could,
so he said the piece of funny poetry all through:

'The Goops they lick their fingers,
And the Goops they lick their knives;
They spill their broth on the tablecloth—
Oh, they lead disgusting lives!
The Goops they talk while eating,
And loud and fast they chew;
And that is why I'm glad that I
Am not a Goop—are you?'

"Good! You've got a very good memory. Now,
Jo, would you get the Bibles for our reading, please."

Joanna went to the sideboard to collect the Bibles,
and looked at the Bible reading notes to see where
the place was.

"We start reading the Acts of the Apostles today,
Daddy."

"Whose turn is it to read?" Mr. Price asked.

"Mine," answered Stephen, holding out his hand
for a Bible.

"Right. Verses one to eleven, then. Afterwards
I'll ask some questions, to see if you've understood."

Stephen read the passage through carefully. At
the end, Mr. Price said, "Will you read the last three
verses again, please?"

So Stephen read, "And when he had said this, as they were looking on, he was lifted up; and a cloud took him out of their sight. And while they were gazing into heaven as he went, behold, two men stood by them in white robes, and said, 'Men of Galilee, why do you stand looking into heaven? This Jesus, who was taken up from you into heaven, will come in the same way as you saw him go into heaven.' "

"Ready for questions?"

"Yes, Dad."

"Where did Jesus go?"

"Into heaven."

"Your turn, Steve. What did the angels say to the disciples?"

"They asked them why they stood looking up into heaven."

"Was that all?"

"No; they said that Jesus would come again just as He left them—or at least, I think that was what they said."

"Yes, you're right. What about Robert? Where is Jesus now?"

Robert said nothing for a while, as if he was afraid he might be wrong. "In heaven?" he asked.

"Yes, in heaven."

"How do you know that there's a place called heaven?" Stephen asked.

"Well, the Bible tells me so, of course, and Jesus told us too."

Joanna had often thought about heaven, but she couldn't really imagine it. "What does Jesus do in heaven?"

"The Bible doesn't tell us much about that. Jesus said that He went to prepare a place in heaven for everyone who trusts in Him. And we know that He remembers us, and helps us when we pray. You are full of questions this morning!"

When Mr. Price said this, it only made Stephen want to ask more!

"Will Jesus really come again, Daddy?"

"I'm sure He will. He promised, 'I will come again,' Can Jesus break a promise, do you think, Robert?"

"No, Uncle."

Mr. Price went on. "The early Christians were sure that Jesus would come back again. When we meet people we often say 'Good morning' or 'Good afternoon'. Instead they would say to one another 'The Lord is coming!' "

"When will it be, Daddy?" Stephen persisted.

"Ah," said Mr. Price. "No one knows except God. No one knows either the day or the hour. It will be unexpected and ever so quick—as quick as blinking your eyes. As suddenly as a burglar robs a house, Jesus will come."

Joanna interrupted. "A girl in our class said that they'd had burglars in their house."

"They didn't expect them, did they?"

"Oh, no, of course not."

"Jesus will come just as suddenly and without people expecting Him."

"Why doesn't He come now, then?" Stephen enquired.

"I can give you only part of the answer to that. When Jesus comes it will be too late for people who've not trusted in Him to do so then. God is so patient that He gives more and more time. But one day He will say that people have had enough time; and then Jesus will come."

"And what's going to happen when Jesus does come?" Joanna joined in.

"Phew!" exclaimed Mr. Price. "What a lot of questions! Well, first of all, we shall see Him."

"And then, Daddy?"

"The Resurrection of the dead will take place."

"What do you mean?"

"Everyone who has believed in the Lord Jesus will be raised from the dead, like Jesus was. He will give them bodies which are just right for heaven. And they will be bodies which will never get ill or wear out. Christians everywhere—whether they are alive or have died—will be gathered together into heaven. It will be like a farmer collecting in all his harvest."

"Is that all, Dad?" Joanna asked.

"No; then will come the judgment. Jesus will reward those who have trusted in Him as Saviour and served Him. And He will punish those who haven't. So some people will be very happy, and others will be sad. But it's time we had our prayer, isn't it?"

"One more question, Daddy, please," begged Stephen. "What will happen to the world then?"

"The Bible says that in the end the world and all that is in it will be burned up and destroyed. And there will be a new world altogether to take its place."

"It's exciting, isn't it?"

"Yes, it is, Steve; very. Now, let's pray together, shall we?"

Then Mr. Price prayed, thanking God for the Lord Jesus, and for the promise that one day Jesus will return.

*   *   *

Saturday morning was lovely and sunny, but in the afternoon the clouds began to gather and grew quite dark. And it wasn't long before it began to pour with rain.

"Just look at it, Mum. What can we do?" asked Stephen.

"Jo and I had an idea while we were out shopping this morning. We bought some coloured spills, just in case. Here!"

"Oh!" exclaimed Stephen, with interest. "Like we had once before when it rained on holiday at the seaside."

"Yes; you can explain to Robert, Steve."

Stephen emptied the spills on to the table. "You

see these coloured spills, Robert—they're thin strips of wood, really. We cut up paper into little squares and we colour them like flags. Then we stick the flags carefully to the top of the spills." Stephen stopped. "Oh, but Mummy, we haven't any glue left!"

Joanna laughed. "Oh, yes, we have! We thought of that—at least, Mummy did."

Mrs. Price smiled. "We bought two bottles. Robert can have one, and you two can share the other. That's if you can share anything without squabbling!"

"I'm going to do what I wanted to do on holiday," said Stephen, "but I couldn't. I think there are pictures of flags in our encyclopaedia."

He went to the book-case and found the right volume. He quickly found the word 'Flags' in the index and turned to the page where they began.

"Look, Dad!" he cried, "there's masses of them—more than a thousand, I should think. Gosh, sixteen whole pages—we'll never manage to do all those!"

Mr. Price peered over his son's shoulder. "Splendid, aren't they? It makes me think how wonderful it's going to be one day."

"What do you mean, Dad?"

"Well, we've been talking about the Lord Jesus coming again. When Jesus comes, He will gather together His people from every nation—from all those countries with flags, and from all the peoples that don't have flags. As you make the flags of the

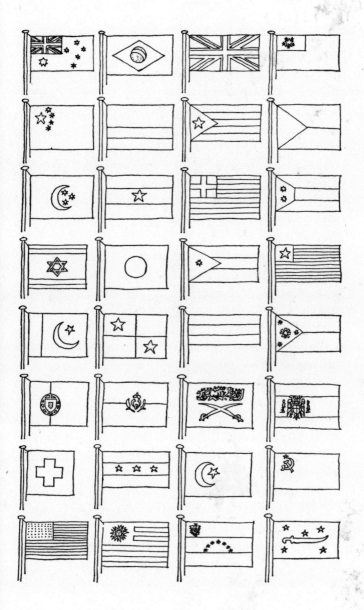

different countries, remember that Jesus wants people in each of them to believe in Him, so that they may be taken to heaven when He comes again."

Robert had already started making his flags, drawing all kinds of patterns. He liked sticking them on to the spills, but he got so much glue on his fingers that as soon as he stuck the flags on, they came off again on his fingers!

Just before tea-time, when they were clearing all their things from the table, there was a ring at the door.

"That's Mummy and Daddy!" shouted Robert and dashed into the hall.

And it was. Robert was so excited he couldn't keep still.

"Hello, Robert. Mmmm, it's good to see you!"

Robert jumped up and down happily, clutching his mother's hand tightly.

"Have you had a good time?"

"Yes, Daddy."

"We've bought the twins a present each because we're sure they've been kind to you."

"Have you brought something for me, too, Mummy?"

His mother and father laughed. "Yes, a game."

"Oh, good! I've learnt lots of games here, Daddy."

"What kind of games?"

"Putting matchsticks on top of milk bottles, marbles, making flags—and, oh, lots of things."

"You *have* had a wonderful time!"

"Can I come again?"

Mrs. Price was glad to hear Robert say that, because she knew then that he had been happy. "Of course you can, Robert. Can't he, twins?"

"Yes, of course, Mum."

"He's nice," said Joanna when the Fysons had left.

"Not bad," said Stephen. "For a four-year-old, that is."

And they all went in to have tea, with lots and lots of lovely shortbread biscuits, all the way from Scotland.